Simply Couponing

"A Couponista's Guide to Savings"

By: Shaliece Matthews Felder

Simply Couponing
A Couponista's Guide to Savings
© 2011 Shaliece Matthews Felder

To address all inquiries or to book a seminar email:
SimplyCouponing@yahoo.com

Editor: Kimberly Kafele

Table of Contents

Acknowledgements

I thank God for the inspiration and insight He's given me in helping my family live our best lives. I am thankfully that He has truly blessed/empowered me. Without God I am nothing.

It is rare that you find someone in life who you can truly call your best friend and I am lucky enough to be married to mine. I'd like to thank my husband - Keeshon S. Felder. Thank you for being my Best friend, my Greatest love, my Closest companion, my Biggest supporter, my Strongest motivator, my Loudest cheerer, my Sweetest tear-wiper and my Spirit-mate. I love you more than any words on paper could ever describe.

I have been doubly blessed with two of the cutest, smartest, funniest children ever born.

Jayden, I could have never imagined how it would feel to have my heart walking around outside of my body until you were born. Thank you for teaching me how to be a mom.

Kaylee, I never knew how much love my heart could hold until the day you were born. You made my heart grow in ways I have no idea it could. Thank you both for teaching me how to love beyond myself.

To my mom, Tierney Matthews, thank you for being my greatest role model. I can only pray that I am half the mom to my children that you were to me. You are truly my inspiration.

To my daddy, Manuel Matthews, thank you for being the man in my life from the beginning. You set the bar on what I should have as a princess and what to expect as someone's queen. Love Rae'

To my "Baby" sister, Shari Matthews, thank you for being my Ride or Die Chick. I'm so proud of the young woman you have become and I only see greatness in you.

To my Spiritual Leaders Apostle Timothy & Lady Nykesha Simpson, thank you for all of your direction and support.

Thank you to all my cousins who pushed to compile my knowledge into this manual.

Special thanks to Kimberly Kafele for all her editorial and publication assistance.

Introduction

If you've turn on the news lately, you will see stories about the recession, a slumping economy and record high unemployment rates. You'll also here stories of the increasingly high gas prices. And if you have visited a grocery store lately you may have noticed that all of this has translated into sky-rocketing grocery prices. Families everywhere are faced with trying to provide groceries for themselves and their families without being forced to break the bank. The upside is there are ways to cut back on your grocery bills, even in this downward economy. The steps in this manual can help the average family save $300 to $500 or more on groceries each month. How? Simply Couponing, of course.

I once heard someone say "If you have never used coupons, it's because you have never been broke enough." I giggled but, I'd have to agree to that. Fact is I barely touched a coupon before two years ago. That changed when both my husband and I (who was 8.5 months pregnant with our second child) were laid off within a month of each other. After much prayer and brainstorming, we decided that it was time for us to follow our dreams and work for ourselves. My husband began our first business, and we chose to work with our own funding as capital instead of high interest business loans (another sign of our economy.). With that said anyone who has started a business or even thought about it, can tell you that it requires some serious investment before you see any sizable return.

So I sat down and looked at all our expenses to see where the bulk of our money was going; and wouldn't you know it was our grocery bill. With that in mind, I reached out to my friend, Tonya, who is the ultimate "couponista". I asked her for some tips on helping me to lower that grocery bill. She was gracious enough to send me all her tips and helped me implement them from over 500 miles away. While I had seen her awesome savings time and time again, I had some doubt that I would be able to do that as well. I had so many questions. "How do I begin using coupons and saving money?" and "How will I find time to coupon shop?"

I believed fictitious things like "There are never any coupons of items I like or use." And "Couponing is too confusing. I can save more on buying generic and in bulk." These are all untrue statements. Everyone can do this and it is so much easier than you may think.

Many people don't think about the fact that being careful with your grocery budget and couponing will expand your choices in other areas of your life. Most people have a budgeted amount of money to live on each month, so it makes sense that spending less of that budget on groceries frees that money up to spend on other things.

At the core, couponing is about taking control over your resources and getting the most you can out of your budget. In just a little over a year, I have went from spending $650 a month in grocery shopping to sending about $250 a month. I have built a sizable stockpile and have been able to save up to 96% on my grocery trips on occasions.

I will walk you through the steps I took, so you can begin to do this for yourself.

What It Takes To Cut That Grocery Bill

Ok you are ready to begin your savings. There are some things I'd like you to keep in mind as you start your savings journey. First, you must keep an open mind. This is essential to saving money. You will need to learn to be open to new products as well as new brand names. I promise you once you see the savings, it will be worth it.

Please remember that Rome wasn't built in a day, so don't expect your couponing to be set in stone right way either. Try to take your time and begin small. If you try to take on too much at once, you will most definitely become overwhelmed and want to quit. Start with one store at first; learn how their sales work, what their coupon policy is and how to master their deals. I started with the drugstore CVS. Their deals are pretty basic, and make it easy to stock up on personal care products pretty quickly. Once you have learned a store, you will begin to gain the confidence that will help you conquer another store.

Next you must begin to collect coupons. As you first begin to coupon shop, there will be deals that you don't have coupons for yet. Typically those coupons will be ones that were in inserts a few weeks before you started, but don't be deterred. Begin building and organizing your coupons and soon enough you will have coupons coming out of your ears. Sales always come back around. And when it does you will be ready with your coupons

This is not couponing the way mom or grandma used to do it. Let's scrap the idea that that you must clip coupons from the paper and run to the store and use them. Wait and shop the sales. Read your store's circular and look for the best sale prices on an item and match it with your coupons to save big money.

Think about doing a complete shopping makeover. You will no longer be buying in bulk or generic items. You will not be shopping for the week; but instead you will be shopping to begin your stockpile. If the item is an extremely low price, then it's a great time to stock up on that item. By buying multiples of an item, you will have enough to last you until the next time that item price is low again.

Where Do I Get Coupons

This is an essential place to start your savings journey because without coupons it is impossible to save money on your grocery bill. If you are new to coupon shopping, let me inform you that there are two main types of coupons and you need them both. First, there is the traditional manufacturers coupons found in the weekend newspaper and second, there is the newer digital and printable coupons found on the internet.

Your first step in coupon shopping will be to find a local newspaper and become a subscriber. I subscribe to 3 newspapers. I will explain why I do shortly.

Inside each weekend paper there are "Coupon Inserts". There are 3 major coupon inserts that appear in the weekend papers. They are Smart Source (SS), Red Plum (RP) and Proctor & Gamble (PG).

You will need to call your local newspaper's subscription department and ask them a few essential questions:

1. "What coupon inserts does your paper carry?" Not all papers carry all 3 (Smart Source, Red Plum and Proctor & Gamble)
2. "Do you offer a Sunday only or weekend only subscription?"
3. "Do you offer any discount if I order multiple copies of your Sunday paper?"

I subscribe to a Sunday only subscription for a little under $2 per paper per week. Any thing around that price or less is a good deal. Now again I also subscribe to 3 Sunday newspapers and I suggest you subscribe to 3 or more as well. The reason being is that you will have 3 or more copies of each coupon. With 3 or more copies of coupons you will then be able to stockpile items that become free or cheap with the coupon.

If you're local newspaper subscription costs a little more or your local paper does not carry some of the coupon inserts, you can purchase whole inserts and even clipped coupons from online coupon services and ebay. Most sites ship quickly but make sure you plan ahead so that they arrive before the sale is over.

If paying for coupon inserts isn't an option, there are some other alternatives. Many people ask their family, friends and neighbors to save their unused coupons for them. I have also heard of people "Dumpster Diving" – when you visit your local recycling center and search through the discarded newspapers to look for coupons. While I have not tried this method, I have seen some extreme coupon clippers do this on television.

There are also a few website that offer printable internet coupons. Printable coupons are free and easy. Before being able to print from any source, you will need to download the "printing software" that enables you to print securely at home. The software is free, downloads quickly and is safe for your computer.

These coupons are available to anyone but be mindful that most manufactures limit how many coupons they make available for print. So if you see a coupon that you want, you should print it before those prints reach their limit.

Most coupons print 3 to a page so to maximize your paper usage try to print in multiplies of 3s. To save on ink most major stores will take a printable coupon that is printed in black and white.

Here is a list of some reputable printable coupon websites:

www.coupons.com
www.smartsource.com
www.redplum.com
www.coolsavings.com

Organize Those Coupons

Yes, you are going to need to set up some organization of your coupons. When I first began I was overwhelmed by the amount of coupons that were all over my work area. Since most coupons are small they would end up blowing off my desk on to the floor or my children would play with them. Worst of all since I had them crammed in every space imaginable I would never remember where I put the ones I needed and they would expire. It was pretty bad, but then I was able to find some ways to organize them.

I've heard of many ways to organize coupons but here are the two methods I think are the most popular.

The first is a Coupon Binder – This method requires you to take the time to organize right away and less time organizing when it's time to go shopping. It will take you a few hours each week to sit and clip your coupons.

The actual clipping of the coupons is simple. If you have multiple copies of the insert like I suggested, you will need to lay each page of the insert onto a table and then place the matching copies of that page on top of each other. So in the end you should have a stack of each page, i.e. four copies of page 1 in a pile, four copies of page 2 in a pile, etc. Then you can staple each individual pile to make it easier to hold together and begin clipping. When clipping always make sure that you never cut off the barcode or Expiration date. Most coupons cannot be used without these in place.

With this method you can use baseball card holders to place your clipped coupons in the binder. You can find them at stores like Walmart, Staples, Target, etc.

You can either divide your binder into categories, by the aisles of your favorite store or alphabetically. I like to divide my binder into categories.

Here is a list of the categories I use in my binder:

- Baby
- Baking
- Beauty
- Beverages
- Breakfast
- Canned Goods
- Cleaners
    - Air Fresheners
    - Dish Soap
    - General
- Cold Meds/First Aid
- Condiments/Sauces
- Feminine Hygiene
- Fruits/Veggies
- Freezer
- Laundry
- Paper Products
- Personal Care
    - Body Wash/ Soaps
    - Deodorants
    - Lotion
    - Oral Care
    - Skin Care
- Pets
- Prepared Side/Pasta/Rice
- Refrigerated
- Snacks – Salty
- Snacks – Sweet
- Miscellaneous

The second method is Filing by Date – This method requires less time to organize your coupons right away, but more time when it comes time to go shopping. You do not clip the coupons right away. Instead you file the entire insert whole. You write the date on the insert and then file them in a file folder. You can label your folders SS, RP & P&G for each inset. This method only requires a few minutes to write the date and file each insert. However all of your clipping and deal organization will happen when you want to go shopping.

Anatomy of a Coupon

Let's break down what a coupon is and how it works. I am a person who likes to have all the information before I start something. I believe knowing how coupons work will give you more confidence in using them correctly to get the maximum savings.

Let's talk about the different parts of coupons.

Expiration Date: All coupons have an expiration date. Some have an expiration date that actually says "No expiration date." Stores usually will not accept coupons that do not have expiration dates. You can use the coupon through the date of the expiration date.

Value: This simply tells you how much will be deducted from your purchase. If it says "Save $1 on 2 boxes of pasta" then you will save $1 total on your purchase of the two boxes (not $1 per box).

Text: This is the most important part of the coupon. It is how you know what the coupon is intended for. If the coupon says "save on ANY xyz product" then it truly can be used on any, not just what is pictured.

Picture: The picture on the coupon can be useful if you have never heard of the product, and can help you locate the item on the shelf. The picture helps build product recognition and is a great form of advertising for the manufacturer. The picture is not what is important though. The manufacturer's generally put the newest or most expensive product in the picture, obviously hoping you will buy that product. As long as you follow what is in the wording of the coupon, you can usually get the lowest priced product which is generally the better deal.

Fine Print: The fine print is usually information for the retailers including the coupon redemption address. There are usually one or two lines that are intended for the consumer though. Here are some examples below:

- Limit one coupon per _purchase_. Each qualifying item(s) is a purchase. If the coupon is for $1 off 2 boxes of cereal and you buy 2 boxes, that is 1 purchase. If you bought 2 more, that is another purchase and you can use another $1/2 coupon. It simply means you can not use 2 coupons on 1 product.
- Limit one coupon per _transaction_. This means you can only use one of each coupon per transaction. Each transaction is concluded with a receipt.
- Limit one coupon per _day/visit_. You can only use one of those coupons per store visit.
- Limit one coupon per _person/customer/household_. You can only use one of these coupons.

What's In a Bar Code

In the picture below you can see a basic coupon bar code. Most coupon bar codes are comprised of five parts and a total of 12 digits.

Bar Code Break Down

Coupon Number Systems Character (NSC): The first digit of a coupon UPC which tells the Point of Sale system that the U.P.C. being scanned is a coupon. It is usually the number "5". The number "9" is another coupon prefix. The "9" is used for non-doubling coupons. If your coupon begins with a "5" then it will automatically double (if your store doubles coupons). If it begins with a "9" then it will not double.

Manufacturer ID: The next 5 digits of the bar code after the NSC is the Manufacturer ID. This number simply a way for manufacturers to speed up the processing of the coupon upon redemption.

Family Code: The next 3 digits are the Family Code. These are assigned by the Manufacturer to "group" products within a "family" together, such as items that are under one brand and are the same size but maybe different varieties.

Value Code : The last 2 digit number is the Value Code that actually identifies the value of the coupon. Example: In most Buy One Get One (BOGO) Free coupons, the value code will be either "01" or "14". If the Value Code is "01" that mean "Free Merchandise", so in turn that coupon is only attached to the free item leaving you free to use an additional coupon on the purchased item. Or it will "14" which means "Buy One Get One Free", that means this coupon is attached to both the purchased item and the free item.

Check Digit - The final digit is the Check Digit. The Check Digit is calculated from all the other digits in the bar code symbol and it changes as the Coupon Code Number changes. It is always in the bar code symbol, in the bars and spaces, and, it is also required in the human readable interpretation under the bar code. Scanners use the Check Digit to ensure that the numbers it has read are the correct numbers.

I must address the fact that there are some people who are deciphering the bar code on a coupon to see if it will work on different (preferably less expensive) items. Please note that the bar code of a coupon is not the intent of the coupon. The bar code is merely a way to speed up the processing of the coupon. No matter what the bar code says, it is the text of the coupon that is the offer. Taking advantage of a glitch in the bar code to get around the text of the coupon is wrong and considered fraud.

You may notice there is an additional barcode on some of your coupons. This is the UCC/EAN Coupon Extended Code. The Joint Industry Coupon Committee has determined that there is a need to bar code additional information not contained in the current Coupon Code. Information such as Offer Codes and Expiration Dates can now be included in bar code symbols for coupons. This can be done through the use of the standard Coupon Extended Code.

Before You Head Out With Your Coupons

Now that we have established how to obtain, organize and decipher our coupons, it's time to talk about how to use them. There are many people who are honestly just trying to say money but inadvertently use coupons incorrectly. And a consistent misuse of coupons can result in stores changing their coupon policies and possibly limiting the use of coupons.

The some important rules when using coupons:

Use Each Coupon As It Is Proposed – Make an effort to always use your coupons how they were intended to be used. If a coupon reads "$1 off 1 Crest Pro Healthy Sensitive Toothpaste" do not try to use it on Crest 3D White Toothpaste. If the coupon reads "$1 off 1 Crest Toothpaste" then you are able to use it on any Crest toothpaste item.

You should always be mindful of the expiration date and any size limitations or restrictions on the coupon as well.

The Value of a Coupon – You should also be mindful of the value of a coupon. If the coupon states "$1 off 2" then you can only use one coupon for the 2 items.

Never Copy a Coupon - This is a major foul in the coupon game. You can NOT copy a coupon. This is considered coupon fraud and is illegal. Most of the time, you can print 2 internet coupons per computer. If I need more than 2, I will use my husband's computer as well or as a family member or friend to print it.

Fraudulent Coupons – If you happen to come across a coupon and you are unsure if it is fraudulent, you can visit the website www.cents-off.com to verify it. They have compiled a list of coupons that have been reported as fraudulent. Never use a fraudulent coupon.

If we all try diligently to use our coupons as they were intended and have a clearer knowledge of our coupons, it will create easier shopping experiences of us as well as our stores. Francis Bacon said "knowledge is power" but any Couponer will tell you "knowledge is savings."

What Is A Catalina Coupon?

Many people have no idea what a Catalina is. I'm sure many of you have been handed a Catalina with the receipt from your transaction but are unsure of what it is.

A Catalina coupon is a coupon that prints out of the Catalina machine. These machines are located right next to the cash registers. Here are some of the different things you can expect to come out of the Catalina Machine:

- Manufacturer coupons - Standard manufacturer coupons print from the Catalina machines but these are always store specific and can only be used at either that particular store or another store takes competitor coupons.

- Store coupons - Store coupon will print from the Catalina machine. Most store coupons which can be stacked with manufacturer coupons.

- Money off coupons - These are coupons that are part of a Catalina deal such as buy 5 products and get $10 back. Or buy $40 in product and get $10 back. These are good on your next shopping trip to the store.

- Deals - Deals that are scheduled in the near future will sometimes print out a Catalina letting you know it is coming.

You should always make sure the Catalina machine is working. Typically you will see a green light on the machine before you begin your transaction. If you were expecting a Catalina deal that day and it doesn't print, you should go to customer service. If the deal is advertised in your store's circular, most customer service workers will be about to handle it right there at the store. If it's an unadvertised deal, you will have to contact the Catalina Company directly via email: Coupons@catalinamarketing.com.

How To Save The Most With Coupons

Everyone I speak to always asks me how to save the most money. It really is easy. I spend my Sunday evenings matching my coupons with the sale ad circulars to all my local stores. Remember that you do not have to use a coupon just because you have it. Hold on to it and match it with an upcoming sale at a store. Here is one simple equation:

Sales
+Store coupon
+ Manufacturers coupon
= Super Cheap Prices.

Some other key things to do to ensure you receive super cheap pricing

First you must join your store's rewards/ loyalty program, i.e. CVS Extra Care Rewards, Rite Aid Wellness Rewards or ShopRite Price Plus Club. These are instant savings and rewards from the store, without clipping a coupon.

Once you've done that you must then learn your store's coupon policy, i.e. double/triple coupons, competitor coupons, limit of coupons per item (my ShopRite only will let me use 4 of the same coupon in one transaction). Each store is different so don't be afraid to ask for a copy to keep up.

You must plan. Review your store's weekly sales circular and use it to plan your weekly shopping trip based on sale items. It takes practice but eventually it becomes easier to pick up great sales.

Try to be as flexible as possible about brands. Sometimes some of the best sales are on items that you may have never purchased in the past. I would have never bought Aquafresh Extreme Clean toothpaste but I grabbed it one day because with a coupon it was free. Lo and behold, I love the way it foams and cleans my teeth.

Like the equation in the beginning of this section you must use store coupons with manufacturer coupons for the best savings. (You can never use 2 manufacturer coupons on 1 item but most stores will allow you to use 1 store and 1 manufacturer coupon on the same item).

Example:
Kellogg's Crunchy Nut Cereal Sale Price- $2.00
Store Coupon $1/1
Manufacturer Coupon $1/1
Final Price: FREE

Know Your Store's Sale Cycles

A good way to get the most out of your match ups is to know your stores sale cycles. Like I mentioned before, you want to hold your coupons until you can match them with the store sales. There are certain items I never pay for as well as others that I won't pay over $1 for.

Things I only buy when they are FREE:

Toothpaste
Toothbrush
Razors
Cheap Deodorant
Shaving Cream
Paper Plates
Plastic Cups
Pain Meds
Cough Medicine
Juice
Popcorn
Salad Dressing
BBQ Sauce

Let me say that it is impossible to get everything for free, but I try to get it super cheap. So if you can not get it free, that's okay but try to figure out a price point that you don't want to pay more than for each item. You may have to wait, but the sale and coupon match up will come around.

Things I will not pay more than $1 for:

Bread
Cereal
Body Wash
Lotion
Cake Mix
Frosting in a can
Laundry Detergent

Pasta Sauce
Paper Towels
Fruit Snacks
Pancake Syrup
Deodorant
Butter
Cleaning Supplies

With that said, it's nice to know about when certain items will be on sale. To help me with that I began creating a price book. This is the method I used to track prices of all the different items I consistently buy.

I know it sounds like work. Who wants to take the time to sit and write down tons of prices? It could only be a few cents difference right? Wrong. Let's go through this: On a typical shopping trip you might buy 40 to 50 items. Now what if you are overpaying for at least 10 of those items? Even if the price difference is only $.40 per item, which is $4 that you didn't really have to spend on that trip. Odds are if you are like most shoppers you are overpaying on more than 10 items and the differential is dollars not just $.40. Knowing your prices gives you the control to be an astute shopper and know whether it's time to stock up or time to walk away from a sale.

To begin your price book gather the receipts from your last three to four shopping trips. Circle the 20 most expensive items you bought on each trip, make sure that they are typical items you buy each week and not a specialty item you just picked up once. Divided your page into seven columns and label them, Item, Store, Date, Brand, Total Price, Size and Unit Price.

Once you have your price book set up with at least 20 items, you can begin to expand it. Try to add 5-10 items to your book per week using the same system you set it up with. Don't feel pressured to expand your price book too fast. No need in overwhelming yourself on something that is supposed to be helpful for you.

Ready to start saving now but don't have a price book yet? Here are some of the sale cycles in my price book.

January – Cereal, Oatmeal, Diet Food, Chips, Dips, Sandwich Items, Wings, Cold and Flu Medicines. Produce: Oranges, Tangerines, Broccoli, Cauliflower, Leeks, Spinach.

February – Canned Food, Oatmeal, Waffles, Chocolate, Personal Lubricants, Asian Sauces/Condiments, Asian Noodles. Produce: Broccoli, Carrots, Papayas, Collards, Avocados.

March – Frozen Foods: Pizza, Ice Cream, Waffles, Seafood, Convenience Meals, Desserts. Produce: Carrots, Pineapples, Rhubarb, Celery, Cabbage.

April – Hams, Eggs, Sugar, Baking Mixes, Organic Foods, Cleaning Items, Seasonal Allergy Medicines. Produce: Artichokes, Beets, Lettuce, Peas, Carrots.

May – Salsa, Tortillas, Charcoal, Ketchup, BBQ Sauces, Chips, Sunscreen, Paper Goods. Produce: Asparagus, Green Beans, Cherries, Onions, Raspberries

June – Dairy: Milk, Yogurt, Eggs, Butter, Ice Cream, Cheese. Produce: Cantaloupe, Apricots, Honeydew Melon, Peaches, Tomatoes, Strawberries, Watermelon.

July - Hot Dogs, Hamburgers, Charcoal, Chips, Dips, Condiments. Produce: Pears, Cucumbers, Nectarines, Peaches, Summer Squash.

August – Breakfast foods: Cold Cereal, Juice, Waffles. Produce: Corn, Onions, Peaches, Plums, Tomatoes.

September – Spaghetti Sauce, Lunch Meat, Pudding Cups, Fruit Snacks, Peanut Butter and Jelly. Produce: Apples, Cucumbers, Spinach, Potatoes, Pumpkins.

October – Candy, Chocolate Chips, Canned Pumpkin, Dog Food, Seafood. Produce: Apples, Cranberries, Yams, Pumpkins, Parsnip.

November – Canned Soups, Stuffing Mixes, Gravy Mixes, Nuts, Canned Milks, Cake Mixes, Frozen Pies. Produce: Yams, Pears, Lemons, Carrots, Squash.

December – Turkey, Egg Nog, Dinner Rolls, Cake Mixes, Hot Chocolate Mixes, Whipped Cream. Produce: Broccoli, Grapefruit, Oranges, Tangerines, Cauliflower.

Ins and Outs of Double Coupons

So you now you have all your coupons clipped and ready to go to the store. You've read your store circular, know the sale cycles and have your match ups. But when reading your coupons you see that some of them say "Do Not Double or Triple". Let's talk about this.

First, what are double coupons? It means the store will match the price of your coupon, for example if you have a manufacturer coupon for $.50, the store will take an additional $.50 off.

Next you will need to find out your store's coupon policy. Many stores offer double coupons. There are times when the same chain of stores may have different double coupons policies, i.e. my local ShopRite doubles all coupons up to $1 but the ShopRite in the next town over only doubles coupons up to $.99.

So how do you know if a coupon will double? All coupons have a UPC code on them that determines if it will double or not. If a coupon has the number 5 as the first number in the UPC code of the coupon, that coupon will double at the cash register. If a coupon has the number 9 as the first number, then it will NOT double at the cash register because it is coded not to do so.

Pretty straight forward. Now let's say you are planning your shopping trip and you have a coupon with the number 5 as the first number of the UPC, meaning it will double at the cash register but it clearly states "Do Not Double" on the top. Will it or won't it double?

Well that is store specific. If you are going to a store that doubles coupons, the doubled part of the coupon is considered a "store coupon". That means the store absorbs the doubled part of the coupon, not the manufacturer.

Example:
$.50 Coupon – the manufacturer covers the cost of that portion of the coupon
$.50 Doubled - the store covers the cost of that portion of the coupon.
Total coupon price deducted - $1.00

There are cases where the manufacturer will cover the full amount of the doubled coupon but that is an arrangement that must be agreed upon between the manufacturer and the store. So when a coupon says "Do Not Double" that means that the manufacturer will not cover the doubled portion of the coupon, so it is up to the store to determine if they will still double it or not. Most stores still double them but there are some that choose not to cover that cost.

What Is a Stockpile

Stockpile, noun: a large supply of food gathered and held in reserve for use during a shortage or during a period of higher prices.

The idea of stockpiling is at the times when we are able to purchase items for cheap or free, it's in our best interest to purchase multiple items of it. Most sales of items go in cycles. The items on sale this week, most likely won't be on sale again for another 2-3 months. So we need to have a supply on hand that will at least last us through that time period so we will not have to buy that item at full price before the next sale comes back around.

This is a good reason to keep that price book I talked about earlier. Knowing when the items you buy frequently are at a good sale price and when the next possible sale price might be are all vital information to stockpiling. You could be stocking up on what appears to be a good price on ground beef, only to find out that if you had waited a week, you could have saved $.50 more a pound.

Finding those great match ups is the secret to you getting your stockpile to a point where you only need to go out to the store each week to buy the items that are at rock bottom prices as well as produce, milk, etc. that are needed on a weekly basis. The larger your stockpile becomes, the less money you will need to spend each week.

If you don't have a lot of time to focus on total stockpiling, focus mainly on the items that you use the most that are the most expensive. Good examples are meat and cereal. When you see a good meat sale, stock-up. This can save you bundles. And when you see a great deal on cereal, stock-up. Cereal is one of the highest marked-up items. Normal cereal can sell for $4 a box but I rarely pay more than $1 a box because I stock up on it when I find a great deal.

There is a long list of items that can be stockpiled but here is a few:

Canned goods (tomatoes, sauce, soups, vegetables)
Cereals
Cleaning supplies (cleaners, garbage bags, laundry det.)
Condiments (BBQ Sauce, steak sauce, mustard, ketchup, mayo)
Dairy (butter, creamers)
Drinks (water, soda, iced tea, coffee, tea, juice)
Health & Beauty Products (shampoo, deodorant, toothpaste, soap, etc)
Rice & Pasta
Meats & Fish (keep frozen)
Paper Products (towels, toilet tissue, plates, napkins)
Snacks (crackers, nachos, salsa, popcorn)

Now, a good stockpile doesn't create itself overnight. It takes quite awhile. A good way to start is to take the extra money you have leftover in your grocery budget each month and to buy up those items that you use the most that are really cheap or free.

Creating a good stockpile at sale prices helps you never have to pay full price for anything. And this can lead to great savings to your budget. Within the first 2 months of starting your stockpile you should start seeing money saved off your grocery bill.

Transforming Savings into a Lower Grocery Bill

Now that you have begun to build a large enough stockpile, the only things you should be purchasing each week are:

- <u>Free Items</u> – You should buy as many as you have coupons for or as many as your store allows. My ShopRite usually has a limit of 4 offers per customer.
- <u>Almost Free Items (nearly 75% off)</u> – If something is extremely cheap and it is something you use or something you may use, than this is a good time to buy it. If it is something you use, you may want to stock up on it.
- <u>Good Sale Items (around 50 – 75% off)</u> – If this is something that you absolutely love, then you should buy it. I do not recommend buying it if it is something you only use occasionally or just want to try it. Those things you get when they are free or almost free (see above.)
- <u>Produce</u> – This is one of the things you cannot stockpile, so you will need to go out and purchase these even once you have a decent stockpile. When shopping for produce, always try to buy what is in season. Also try to learn your local stores price points for them.
- <u>Dairy</u> – There are also some dairy items that are difficult to stockpile such as milk and eggs. Like produce try to know your local store's prices.
- <u>Meats</u> – You can stockpile meats in your freezer but you should still be purchasing meat when you go to the store if it is on sale or they are having a special. The only time I recommend not purchasing more meat is if there is none on sale at a great price that week or your freezer is just too full.

Now keep in mind that every family situation is different, so there may be other factors that you must consider like the size of your family or if there are dietary restrictions that a member of the family has or if you need to purchase diaper or dog food. This all must be taken into account.

Remember saving big dollars off of your grocery bill does take time. I personally spend a few hours a week on couponing – finding, clipping and organizing coupons and preparing my grocery lists for each store.

Getting your stockpile up is the first step to big savings. Once your stockpile is going and you are purchasing only the key items I have listed above, you will begin to see your grocery bill drop more and more each week until you arrive at a budget that is comfortable for your family.

Be On the Lookout for Store Deals That Don't Need Coupons

Gasp! No coupons? Believe it or not, you can actually get pretty good deals on items at the store without coupons. (Though, the coupons do sweeten the deals.) You just have to keep your eyes open as you shop.

For example, there was a deal a few weeks back on Coke. When you buy 5 Coke products for $11, you'll get 2 Hillshire Farms lunch meats for FREE. No coupons needed. No Catalinas. It's just deducted automatically on your order. Talk about a good deal. Grocery stores run deals like this all the time.

By keeping your eyes open and buying up deals for the items you use the most will help you save money on your grocery budget.

Rain Checks

So you are all excited about a sale and you run to the store to pick it up but it seems like everyone else was excited about the same sale. Your store is completely out of the item. So now what?

Rain Check!!

They are so under-utilized and one of the best kept secrets. A Rain Check is a slip of paper that you ask a store for when they are out of an item that is on sale. This slip of paper allows you to return to the store when the item is back in stock and purchase it at the sale price. Some stores have an expiration date on the rain check and others do not. Some stores even have a maximum quantity amount per item.

When using your Rain Check, be sure to check that the coupon you planned on using won't expire before the item is stocked again in the store. Also be sure to mention to the cashier that you are using a Rain Check before they start your transaction. They will have to manually key in the price of the items you are purchasing.

Smooth Checkout Transactions

Now is the moment when it all comes together. You are ready to check out and see those savings. Here are a few tips to making your transaction go smoothly.

Be Organized

You may want to get organized before you enter a store

- I make a list of the things I want to buy.

- If I'm buying participating items as part of a Catalina promotion and I like to separate my transactions, I make a separate list for each transaction.

- I usually pull out all the coupons I am using on that trip and place them into an envelope.

- Sometime you may not pick up all the items on your list that you have coupons for. That's ok but be sure to have the ones you are using ready before you checkout.

Be Kind

- Upon checkout I usually smile and make conversation with the cashier. (Don't worry about the grumpy ones that choose not to engage.)

- I inform my cashier that I have coupons and ask if they would like them before or after they scan my items.

- If I have multiple transactions usually I may let the person behind me go ahead.

- I always tell the person behind me that I have a ton of coupons and if they are in a hurry, they may want to choose a different line. Most times they go to a different line but other times they stay ask me about the coupons I am using. That becomes a teachable moment for me.

- Occasionally I will get the person behind me that will not move and they will roll their eyes or make snide comments. I always ignore them! I love saving money and that feeling supersedes any guilt they try and push on me.

Be on the Watch

- Always watch the checkout screen to ensure that your items ring up the prices that they should and to ensure that your coupons take off the amount they should. If you missed something inform your cashier and ask them to show it to you.

- Do not be afraid to ask for a member of management to come clarify something for you. Often, you know more about the store coupon policy then the checkers, so don't be afraid to nicely ask for a manager to explain something to you.

- Always have a copy of the store's coupon policy with you! Most times you will need to have this on hand to show the cashier if there is a dispute in what the policy is.

Be Prepared to Walk Away From a Deal

- There are times when some cashiers or even managers refuse to honor their coupon policy as it is written. It is never worth an argument, so on those occasions you have to be prepared to walk away from the deal.

Tips For Shopping At Chain Drug Stores

There are 3 major chain drug store in the US – Walgreens, CVS and Rite Aid.

Walgreens

Walgreens is the largest national drugstore chain in the US. It operates over 7000 stores across all 50 US states. Walgreens runs register rewards promotions each week, I will explain that further. Their sale cycles run Sunday-Saturday.

As mentioned above, Walgreens rewards their shoppers with Register Rewards. Register rewards (commonly called RRs) are coupons from the Catalina machine that print after you make a qualifying purchase. Most RRs are what we couponers call "On Your Next Order" (OYNO) which can be used like cash on your next order (this could be the very next order you are making at the register).

Sometimes you may receive a Catalina coupon for money off a particular item or an advertisement for a current or future register reward deal.

How do you receive a Register Reward?

Buy the exact items advertised to receive the RR. Using coupons on these items will not affect whether your RR prints. If it doesn't print, it is likely because the Catalina machine isn't working. Insist that the cashier ring you on another register if your RR doesn't print and you know it should have.

If you complete more than one register rewards deal in one transaction, one reward for each different RR deal should print. You will NOT receive more than one RR for the same RR deal in the same purchase. If you want to purchase multiple identical items, you will need to complete separate transactions.

If you purchased the right items and didn't get a RR, you can return the items on the spot or call the Catalina company. They'll be able to see if the machine was working and if you bought the right products. It does tend to take a few minutes for the call and then you have to wait to get the RR which takes 6 – 8 weeks.

How do you spend a Register Reward?

Generally, you can use your RR just like cash on your next purchase, but of course there are exceptions:

Most RR's explicitly say that it cannot be used on tobacco, alcohol, tax, lottery tickets, money orders, stamps, dairy, or any gift cards or pre-paid cards.

As stated in the fine print, you cannot use more RR's and manufacturer coupons than number of items you are buying. This is what is called "coupon to item ratio". As long as you are buying as many items as you have RR & manufacturer coupons, you should be able to use more than one RR. Store coupons do not affect how many manufacturer and RR's you can use. If you don't have enough items, grab something for a quarter or less and use your RR for that item. The amount doesn't matter. Example: If you are buying (3) bottles of Suave shampoo and have (3) $0.50 coupons and 1 RR for $2 that you want to use to pay for these items. Since you have a total of 4 coupons according to the register (they count an RR as a coupon), the register will beep when the 4th coupon is scanned and you won't be able to use it. In order to use it, you will need to purchase a 4th item called a filler. This can be any item in the store and can cost anywhere from 1c and up. I usually get a cheap piece of candy.

You cannot "roll" RR's into the same deal 99% of the time. So if you buy an item and it earns an RR, you cannot use that RR to pay for a second identical item and get an RR for that one as well.

Example: If you use an RR from purchasing a bottle of Suave to pay for your purchase of a second bottle of Suave, you will NOT get another RR. The best way to "roll" is to use your Suave RR to pay for a different RR deal. You can then use the RR's from the 2nd deal, to purchase more Suave.

Please check the Walgreens website for their entire coupon policy.

CVS

CVS is the second largest national drugstore chain in the US. It operates approximately 7000 stores in 45 states. CVS sale cycles run Sunday-Saturday

First you will need to get CVS ExtraCare card. This card will enable you to get sale prices and earn Extra Care Bucks. You can ask a cashier for an application or sign up online. It's a good idea to get one at the store so you can have your card right away.

Before you do any shopping when you arrive at your CVS, always go to the kiosk and scan your card. The "magic coupon machine" as some couponers like to call it, will give you store coupons that are good for a certain length of time. Some are only good that day so always be sure to check the dates.

CVS gives you rewards when you purchase advertised items called Extra Bucks (ECB). The ECB will print at the end of your receipt. Make sure that you clip them and keep up with them. If you lose them, they will not be replaced.

Some things to keep in mind regarding ECB:

- The required amount to receive the ECB is always calculated before coupons.
- ECB can be used to purchase nearly anything in the store. (excluding prescriptions, alcohol, Gift Cards, lottery, money orders, postage stamps, pre-paid cards

and tobacco products, as printed on the ECB.) They also cannot be used to pay the tax on a transaction.

- You cannot get change back when you spend your ECBs. However, they can be entered as less than their face value, for example if your total (before tax) comes to $1.97 and you have an ECB for $1.99 that you would like to use and you don't mind losing 2 cents of its value, the cashier will adjust the value to the balance due before tax.
- ECBs expire 4 weeks from the date they are printed.

Using coupons at CVS:

- CVS accepts manufacturer's coupons including internet printable coupons.
- CVS also issue their own store coupons. You can get these through CVS emails (make sure that your email address is listed with your card online), printed out at the end of your receipt (these are referred to as CRT's – cash register tape coupons), or at the magic coupon machine. Sometimes coupons are also located in the sales flyer.
- Both ECBs and CRT coupons are linked to your CVS card. This means you cannot use them without the same CVS card that earned them.
- CVS coupon policy allows for the use of one manufacturer and one CVS coupon on each item. ECB are not counted as coupons in this respect, you may use as many of these as you like.

Please email CVS for their entire coupon policy.

Rite Aid

Rite Aid is the third largest national drug store chain in the US. It operates more than 4900 stores in 31 states. Rite Aid offers a Single Check Rebate program, +Up Rewards program and distributes coupons via Rite Aid Ad Perks. You can create an account to participate in these programs. Most Rite Aid sales run Sunday-Saturday.

Single Check Rebates:

SCR stands for Single Check Rebate, Rite Aid's monthly rewards/rebate program. Just register online and you can immediately start participating. Each month Rite Aid publishes a booklet that highlights these deals.

Throughout the month as you make purchases, enter your receipt information on the website or keep an envelope for mail submissions. At the end of the month, you can request your rebate by clicking the "request rebate" button. Do NOT request the rebate if you are planning to make any more rebate purchases that month as you are only allowed one submission per month.

Check the limitations for the items you are expecting rebates on. Most of the SCR rebates are limited to one item per household. Also, you'll want to take note of the rebate dates. Many of the rebates are valid for just a week and not the entire month. Also sometimes an SCR cycle straddles two months.

If you have a coupon for an item that is free after rebate (FAR) then definitely use it. You will get the full purchase price back. If you use a coupon for that item, you've just made a profit for your fund!

+Up Rewards:

Look for +Up Reward items throughout the weekly circular. When you use your Wellness+ card, the +Up Rewards will print on the end of your receipt and you can use them to buy another product in the store (excluding prescriptions, tobacco, alcohol, etc). Make sure you note when they expire and treat them just like cash.

Wellness+ rewards

Rite Aid has a new program called Wellness+ where you earn points for your purchases. You will need to apply for your card. You will get a temporary card and the permanent one will be mailed to you. There are tons of rewards available with this program. Like for every 125 points (up to 375) one-time, you will receive 10% off shopping pass. There are some everyday benefits you'll enjoy as well such as members-only sale pricing throughout the store and 10% of Rite-Aid brand products every day. To find out all of the ways to save at Rite Aid you should check out their website.

Using store coupons at Rite Aid

Many times Rite Aid offers money off total purchase coupons (like a $5 off $25 purchase). These are awesome coupons to have because they are applied before the store and manufacturer coupons.

One way to get money off of total purchase coupon is by viewing the video values coupons. Just view 20 short videos advertising different products and you will get one of these coupons, plus extra coupons for the item commercials you just viewed. These are Rite-Aid coupons and can be combined with ad coupons and/or manufactured coupons. These are limited to one per customer.

Rite Aid produces its own coupons and releases them either in the weekly flyer or online. These can be stacked with manufacturer coupons. Some stores limit these to one per customer.

Please check the Rite Aid website for their entire coupon policy

What In The World Are You Talking About?

Acronyms & Definitions of terms used in the coupon world.

ACRONYMS:

$1/1, $1/2: One dollar off one item, one dollar off two items, etc.

B1G1/BOGO: Buy one, Get one. This acronym is usually followed by "free" or "half off". This means just that.

CAT: Catalina – See definition

ECB: Extra Care Bucks from CVS program. Now renamed Extra Bucks.

EXP: Expires or Expiration Date

IP: Internet printed coupons that are printed at home.

MFR: Manufacturer

MIR: Mail in rebate. This refers to rebates which must be submitted by mail.

MM: Moneymaker

OYNO: On Your Next Order. Some stores have deals like, Spend $15, save $5 on your next order. This type of savings will need to be redeemed on your next purchase.

OOP: Out of pocket

P&G: Procter & Gamble insert. P&G manufacture a wide range of consumer goods and put out monthly coupon inserts filled with coupons for a variety of their brands.

PP: Price Plus; Savings Club from ShopRite

PSA: Prices Start At

Q: Abbreviation for coupon.

RP: Red Plum Insert. RP is marketing company, like SS, and their inserts and website feature coupons from a variety of manufacturers.

RR: Register Rewards; Walgreens drugstore rewards program, and version of the Catalina coupon.

SCR: Single Check Rebate. Rite Aid Drugstore monthly rebate program.

SS: Smart Source Insert. SS is marketing company, like RP, and their inserts and website feature coupons from a variety of manufacturers.

UPC: Universal Product Code. Bar code printed on product packages that can be scanned electronically.

Wags: Walgreens

WYB: When You Buy. Certain deals or coupons require you to purchase multiple items to score a deal.

YMMV: Your miles may vary. It means that each store, even under the same chain is different and so are their policies.

DEFINITIONS:

Blinkie: Red Smart Source machines found in most stores.

Catalina: They are coupons that print out at the register after your sale is complete. It is a separate machine that is just for printing out coupons or dollars off. Some Catalina's are advertised and some are generated based on consumer behavior.

Coupon Insert: Coupon circulars inserted into Sunday newspapers amongst the other advertisements.

Coupon: a note from a store or manufacturer that gives a shopper a discount on specific product.

Couponing: the art of redeeming coupons in order to save money.

Couponer: A person who collects and saves coupons to redeem them on products.

E-Coupons: Electronic coupons may be downloaded onto your store loyalty card or cell phone.

Manufacturer: A company who produces the brand items.

Manufacturer Coupon: A coupon created by the manufacturer, or by a marketing company on the manufacturer's behalf.

Peelie: An adhesive manufacturer coupon located on an item that you must peel off to redeem.

Purchase: Refers to buying any item.

Raincheck: A written slip that you can request from a store when a sale item is out of stock. When the store restocks the item, after the sale period is over, a rain check entitles you to purchase for the previous sale price. Store may include an expiration date as well as a quantity limit on your rain check. Rain checks are usually issued at the customer service desk.

Rebate: A rebate is a refund of some or the entire amount paid. Rebates are offered and sponsored by a store or a manufacturer. Either clip and mail UPC barcodes or enter receipt proof of purchase online, then wait for your rebate check in the mail.

Stacking: Using any two promotions together.

Stacking Coupons: Using both a store coupon and a manufacturer coupon on one product.

Stockpile: To buy many items at a time in order to build your supply.

Store Coupon: A coupon created by the store to entice you to buy a certain product at their store.

Store Loyalty Card: A free card which you present at checkout to receive additional savings. Fill out a short application to receive a loyalty card at your local grocer.

Tearpad: Coupon pads located in stores to promote products.

HAPPY SAVINGS

~SHALIECE

Visit my blog:

http://simplycouponingguide.blogspot.com/

or come check me out on Facebook:

http://www.facebook.com/SimplyCouponing

www.ingramcontent.com/pod-product-compliance
Lightning Source LLC
Chambersburg PA
CBHW070227290526
45789CB00004B/1529